POC
THERAPY
for
ANXIETY

EDMUND J. BOURNE, PHD
LORNA GARANO

New Harbinger Publications, Inc.

Distributed in Canada by Raincoast Books

Copyright © 2020 by Edmund Bourne and Lorna Garano
         New Harbinger Publications, Inc.
         5674 Shattuck Avenue
         Oakland, CA 94609
         www.newharbinger.com

"Make a Plan to Deal with Worry," page 152, adapted with permission from *The Worry Control Workbook* by Mary Ellen Copeland (2000).

Cover design by Sara Christian; Acquired by Elizabeth Hollis Hansen; Edited by Marisa Solís; Text design by Michele Waters and Amy Shoup

Printed in the United States of America
Library of Congress Cataloging-in-Publication Data on file

Printed in the United States of America

21 20 19

10 9 8 7 6 5 4 3 2 1

First Printing

CONTENTS

INTRODUCTION

This is a book about how to cope with anxiety. It's a little package of practical strategies that will help you better understand—and handle—your anxiety, whatever its form.

Before we get to the strategies, though, this introduction is a quick primer on the nature and types of anxiety.

Anxiety comes in many guises. Understanding more about your particular type of anxiety can help you get a better idea of what you're dealing with. Equally important, understanding where your particular issues with anxiety might have come from—and what causes are likely to keep it going—will help you decide which of the many strategies in this book might help you most.

Anxiety 101

Anxiety is an inevitable part of life in our times. Many situations come up in everyday life where it's appropriate and reasonable to react with some anxiety. The strategies in this book can be of use to anyone experiencing normal, ordinary anxiety reactions (everyone, in other words) as well as those dealing with specific anxiety disorders.

Anxiety affects your whole being. It is a physiological, behavioral, and psychological reaction all at once. On a bodily level, anxiety may involve rapid heartbeat, muscle tension, queasiness, dry mouth, or sweating. On a behavioral level, it can paralyze your ability to act, express yourself, or deal with certain everyday situations. Psychologically, it is a state of apprehension and uneasiness. In its most extreme forms, anxiety can cause you to feel detached from yourself and even fearful of dying or going crazy.

The fact that anxiety can affect you on all these levels means that a complete program of coping with anxiety must address all three components. The cognitive-behavioral skills in this book will teach you to reduce physiological reactivity, eliminate avoidance behavior, and change self-talk that feeds your apprehension and worry.

Anxiety can appear in different forms and at different levels of intensity. It can range in severity from a mere twinge of uneasiness to a full-blown *panic attack* marked by heart palpitations, trembling, sweating, dizziness, disorientation, and terror. Anxiety that is not connected with any particular situation—that comes out of the blue—is called *free-floating anxiety*. In more severe instances, it can manifest as a spontaneous panic attack.

If your anxiety arises only in response to a specific situation, it is called *situational anxiety* or *phobic anxiety*. Situational anxiety is different from everyday worries in that it tends to be out of proportion or unrealistic. If you have a disproportionate apprehension about driving on freeways, going to the doctor, or socializing, this may qualify as situational anxiety. Situational anxiety becomes phobic when you actually start to avoid the situation: you give up driving on freeways, going to doctors, or socializing altogether. In other words, phobic anxiety = situational anxiety + persistent avoidance of the situation.

Often anxiety arises merely by thinking about a particular situation. When you feel distressed about what might happen when you have to face a difficult or even phobic situation, you are experiencing what is called *anticipatory anxiety*. In its milder forms, anticipatory anxiety is indistinguishable from ordinary worry. (*Worrying* can be defined as anticipating unpleasant consequences about a future situation.) But sometimes, anticipatory anxiety becomes intense enough to be anticipatory panic.

There is a difference between spontaneous anxiety/panic and anticipatory anxiety/panic. Spontaneous anxiety tends to come out of the blue, peaks to a high level very rapidly, and then subsides gradually. The peak is usually reached within five minutes, followed by a gradual tapering over an hour or more. Anticipatory anxiety tends to build more gradually in response to encountering or simply thinking about a threatening situation, and may last longer. You may worry yourself into a frenzy about something for an hour or so and then let go of the worry as you tire or find something else to occupy your mind.

Finally, *anxiety disorders* are distinguished from everyday, normal anxiety in that they involve anxiety that is more intense (for example, panic attacks), lasts longer (anxiety that may persist for months instead of going away after a stressful situation has passed), or leads to phobias that interfere with your life. (Criteria for diagnosing specific anxiety disorders have been established by the American Psychiatric Association and are listed in a manual used by mental health professionals called the *Diagnostic and Statistical Manual of Mental Disorders*.)

Causes of Anxiety

Anxiety symptoms often seem irrational and inexplicable, so it's only natural to ask what causes them. Before we detail various causes of anxiety, keep these two general points in mind.

First, although learning about the causes of anxiety can give you insight into how anxiety problems develop, you don't need such knowledge to overcome your particular difficulty. The various strategies for handling anxiety presented in this book do not depend on a knowledge of underlying causes to be effective. However much you may know about causes, this knowledge is not necessarily what cures.

Second, be wary of the notion that there is one primary cause, or type of cause, for either everyday anxiety or anxiety disorders. Whether you are dealing with ordinary anxiety, apprehension about a job interview, panic disorder, or obsessive-compulsive disorder, recognize that there is no one cause that, if removed, would eliminate the problem.

Anxiety problems arise from a variety of causes operating on numerous levels. These levels include heredity, biology, family background and upbringing, conditioning, recent life changes, your self-talk and personal belief system, your ability to express feelings, current environmental stressors, and so on.

The idea that your particular difficulties are "just a brain imbalance" or "just a psychological disturbance" neglects the fact that nature and nurture are interactive. While brain imbalances may certainly be set up by heredity, they may also result from stress or psychological factors. Psychological problems, in turn, may be influenced by inborn biological predispositions. There is simply no way to say which came first or which is the "ultimate" cause.

By the same token, a comprehensive approach to overcoming anxiety, panic, worry, or phobias cannot restrict itself to treating physiological or psychological causes in isolation. A variety of strategies dealing with several different levels—including biological, behavioral, emotional, mental, interpersonal, and even spiritual factors—is necessary. This multidimensional approach to overcoming anxiety is assumed throughout this book.

Targeting Anxiety's "Maintaining Causes"

This book addresses the *maintaining causes* of anxiety. These are the factors in your current behavior, attitude, and lifestyle that keep anxiety going once it has developed. What you'll learn from this book will also affect the neurobiological causes (since mind, behavior, and brain all interact), but more indirectly. The long-term, predisposing causes, including heredity, are more difficult to change. Short of genetic engineering and direct modification of your DNA structure, you cannot change your genes. However, you can certainly change the way you respond to and deal with your genetic predispositions. This book will help you do this.

Recent, circumstantial causes of your difficulties with anxiety have also already happened. Using the strategies in this book will help you better deal with recent as well as long-term stressors you've encountered. Managing the stress in your life—past, recent, or present—will go a long way to help you better cope with everyday anxiety, worry, or specific anxiety disorders.

A Note about Medications

One intervention not covered in this book is medication. Since use of prescription medications is not really a self-help technique, but relies on the expertise of a physician, it has not been included. However, prescription

medications are widely used in helping people
with anxiety, especially those struggling with
more severe cases of anxiety disorders, such
as panic disorder, agoraphobia, obsessive-
compulsive disorder, and post-traumatic
stress disorder.

You can obtain a referral to a psychiatrist
in your area skilled in treating anxiety disorders by contacting the Anxiety and Depression
Association of America at (240) 485–1001 or
going to their website (www.adaa.org) and
clicking on "Find a Therapist."

About This Book

The Pocket Therapy Guide to Anxiety is just
that—a portable companion for you to use
anytime, anywhere you need quick relief or
want to work on new practices and skills.
Take it with you, mark it up, and make it

yours. The last few pages have space for you to take notes on what works.

Each chapter teaches strategies drawn from the most effective evidence-based approaches to anxiety, including cognitive behavioral therapy, acceptance and commitment therapy, mindfulness- and compassion-based approaches, and body-based practices. Chapters 1 through 9 will give you insight into the habits and techniques that work best for you. Chapter 10 contains a first aid kit of ways to cope on the spot when anxiety is high. We suggest you keep a separate notebook or journal to use for some of the exercises or techniques or to write about your insights. You'll also find additional resources at www.newharbinger.com/47612.

1

RELAX YOUR BODY

Anxiety often manifests itself as a cluster of physical symptoms. In fact, when asked to describe their anxiety, many people begin by enumerating a list of disquieting physical sensations, such as shortness of breath, muscle tension, hyperventilation, and palpitations. Such symptoms reinforce anxiety-producing thoughts.

Try to think for a moment of your anxiety as a solely physical condition. What are the symptoms of this condition? How do they affect your sense of well-being? How do you respond to them? Although it may seem like these physical symptoms are automatic reflexes beyond your control, you can take comfort in knowing that they are not. With practice, you can stem the physical effects of anxiety and free yourself from its grip.

Progressive Muscle Relaxation

Progressive muscle relaxation (PMR) is a simple technique used to halt anxiety by relaxing your muscles one group at a time. Its effectiveness was recognized decades ago by Edmund Jacobson, a Chicago physician.

If your anxiety is strongly associated with muscle tension, progressive muscle relaxation will probably prove an especially useful tool for you. This muscle tension is often what leads you to say that you are "uptight" or "tense."

Symptoms that respond well to progressive muscle relaxation include tension headaches, backaches, tightness in the jaw, tightness around the eyes, muscle spasms, high blood pressure, and insomnia. If you are troubled by racing thoughts, you may find that systematically relaxing your muscles tends to slow down your mind. If you take

tranquilizers, you may find that regular practice of progressive muscle relaxation will
enable you to lower your dosage.

There are no contraindications for progressive muscle relaxation unless the muscle
groups to be tensed and relaxed have been
injured. If this is the case, consult your doctor
before attempting progressive muscle
relaxation.

Here are some guidelines for practicing
progressive muscle relaxation (PMR).

- Find a quiet location to practice
  where you won't be distracted.

- Practice at regular times.

- Practice on an empty stomach.
  Food digestion after meals will
  tend to disrupt deep relaxation.

- Assume a comfortable position.
  Your entire body, including your

head, should be supported.
Sitting up is preferable to lying
down if you are feeling tired
and sleepy.

- Let your body be unencumbered.
  Loosen any tight garments and
  take off your shoes, watch,
  glasses, contact lenses, jewelry,
  and so on.

- Make a decision not to worry
  about anything.

- Assume a passive, detached
  attitude. You want to adopt a "let
  it happen" attitude and be free
  of any worry about how well you
  are performing the technique:
  Do not try to relax; do not try to
  control your body; do not judge

your performance. The point is to let go.

- Tense, don't strain. When you tense a particular muscle group, do so vigorously, without straining, for seven to ten seconds.

- Concentrate on what is happening.

- Let go. When you release a particular muscle group, do so abruptly, and then relax, enjoying the sudden feeling of limpness. Allow relaxation to develop for at least fifteen to twenty seconds before going on to the next group of muscles.

- Try repeating a relaxing phrase. You might say to yourself, "I am relaxing," "let go," or "let the tension flow away."

- Maintain your focus on your muscles.

- Practice for at least twenty minutes per day.

The idea is to tense each muscle group hard (but not so hard that you strain it) for about ten seconds, and then to let go of it suddenly. Then give yourself fifteen to twenty seconds to relax, noticing how the muscle group feels when relaxed in contrast to how it felt when tensed, before going on to the next group of muscles. The following exercise gives you step-by-step instructions.

How to Do PMR

Sit or lie down, comfortably supported, in a quiet place. Take three deep abdominal breaths, exhaling slowly each time. As you exhale, imagine the tension throughout your body beginning to flow away.

Start by clenching your fists. Hold for seven to ten seconds and then release for fifteen to twenty seconds. Use these same time intervals for all other muscle groups: biceps, triceps, the muscles in your forehead and face, around your eyes, jaw, and back of your neck.

Then move slowly down to the back of your head and neck. Take a few deep breaths and tune in to the weight of your head sinking into whatever surface it is resting on. Move on to your shoulders, chest, stomach, lower back, buttocks, and thighs. You will probably have to tighten your hips along with your thighs, since the thigh muscles attach at the pelvis. Hold...and then relax. Feel your thigh muscles smoothing out and relaxing completely. Tighten your calf muscles, and then your feet.

Finally, mentally scan your body for any residual tension. If a particular area remains tense, repeat one or two tense-relax cycles for that group of muscles. Now, imagine a wave of relaxation slowly spreading throughout your body, starting at your head and gradually penetrating every muscle group all the way down to your toes.

The entire progressive muscle relaxation sequence should take you twenty to thirty minutes the first time. With practice, you may decrease the time needed to fifteen to twenty minutes.

To download a guided audio meditation for progressive muscle relaxation visit: www .newharbinger.com/47612.

Five More Body-Relaxation Practices

As an alternative to progressive muscle relaxation you may want to try *passive muscle relaxation*, which does not require actively tensing and relaxing your muscles. Progressive muscle relaxation is a bit more "potent medicine" for body tension, but passive muscle relaxation works quite well too. You can download and listen to a guided audio meditation for passive muscle relaxation at www.newharbinger .com/47612.

* * *

As you continue to practice progressive muscle relaxation you will become more adept at recognizing and releasing tension in your muscles. In fact, you may become so attuned to what's happening in your body that you need not deliberately contract each muscle before you relax it. This is called *relaxation without tension*. Instead, scan your body for tension by running your attention through this sequence of four muscle groups: arms, head and neck, shoulders and torso, and legs. If you find any tightness, simply let go of it, just as you did after each contraction in the progressive muscle relaxation exercise.

* * *

In *cue-controlled relaxation*, you learn to relax your muscles whenever you want by combining a verbal suggestion with abdominal breathing. Here's how to do it.

First, take a comfortable position, then release as much tension as you can using the relaxation-without-tension method. Focus on your belly as it moves in and out with each breath. Make breaths slow and rhythmic.

Now, on every inhalation, say to yourself the words "breathe in" and, as you exhale, "relax." Just keep saying to yourself, "Breathe in…relax, breathe in…relax," while letting go of tension throughout your body. Continue this practice for five minutes, repeating the key phrases with each breath. The cue-controlled method teaches your body to associate the word *relax* with the feeling of relaxation.

* * *

The way you breathe directly reflects the level of tension you carry in your body and can aggravate or diminish your anxiety symptoms. Is your breath slow or rapid? Deep or shallow? Does it center around a point high in your chest or down in your abdomen? Do you breathe with your mouth open? You might also take note of changes in your breathing pattern under stress compared to when you are more relaxed.

The following exercise will help you change your breathing pattern. Just three minutes of practicing *abdominal breathing* exercise will usually induce a deep state of relaxation. You can find this and other breathing meditations at www.newharbinger .com/47612.

Abdominal Breathing

- Note the level of tension you're feeling. Then place one hand on your abdomen right beneath your rib cage.

- Inhale slowly and deeply through your nose into the bottom of your lungs; in other words, send the air as low down as you can. If you're breathing from your abdomen, your hand should actually rise.

- When you've taken in a full breath, pause for a moment, and then exhale slowly through your nose or mouth, depending on your preference. Be sure to exhale fully. As you exhale, allow your whole body to just let go.

- Do ten slow, full abdominal breaths. Try to keep your breathing smooth and regular, without gulping in a big breath or letting your breath out all at once.

- After you've slowed down your breathing, count from twenty down to one, counting backward one number with each exhalation. If you start to feel light-headed while practicing abdominal breathing, stop for fifteen to twenty seconds and breathe in your normal way, then start again.

- Five full minutes of abdominal breathing will have a pronounced effect on reducing anxiety or early symptoms of panic.

Finally, a *yoga practice* can be instrumental in easing your body's tension. The word *yoga* means "to yoke or unify." By definition, yoga seeks to promote unity of mind, body, and spirit. Although in the West, yoga is usually thought of as a series of stretching exercises, it actually embraces a broad philosophy of life and an elaborate system for personal transformation.

Many people find that yoga simultaneously increases energy and vitality while calming the mind. Yoga may be compared to progressive muscle relaxation, in that it involves holding the body in certain flexed positions for a few moments and then relaxing. Like vigorous exercise, yoga directly promotes mind-body integration. In recent decades, yoga has become a very popular method for reducing anxiety and stress. We recommend giving it a try.

2

RELAX YOUR MIND

From the time we wake up until we fall asleep, we are engaged in an almost constant mental bustle. Anxiety may accelerate this so that you feel like your mind is racing and you're bombarded with thoughts. If you're like many Westerners, the idea of maintaining a daily regimen designed to relax your mind and induce serenity may sound foreign to you. But some of these techniques have endured for centuries and are now practiced the world over.

Guided Visualization

Guided visualization is a method of deliberately using mental imagery to modify your behavior, the way you feel, and even your internal physiological state. You can consciously create visualizations or mental sense impressions as a preventive measure against anxiety. When you practice guided visualization, you will close your eyes and imagine yourself in a calming scenario.

Here are some guidelines for practicing guided visualization.

- Get into a comfortable position, free of encumbrances and with your head supported.

- Make sure that your environment is quiet and free from distractions.

- Give yourself time to relax before undertaking a guided visualization. To this end, you can use progressive muscle relaxation or abdominal breathing for a few minutes before you start.

- At the conclusion of your relaxing visualization, bring

yourself back to an alert state of mind with the following statements: *"Now, in a moment, you can begin to come back to an alert, wakeful state of mind. Pay attention as I count from one up to five. When I get to five, you can open your eyes and feel awake, alert, and refreshed. One… gradually beginning to come back to an alert, wakeful state. Two… more and more awake. Three… beginning to move your hands and feet as you become more alert. Four… almost back to a fully alert state. And five… opening your eyes now, finding yourself fully awake, alert, and refreshed."*

• After finishing with your visualization, get up and walk

around a bit until you feel fully
alert and grounded.

- Allow at least ten minutes to
  pass before driving a car or
  engaging in any other activity
  that requires complex
  coordination.

Below is a guided visualization you can
use to relax your mind when you feel tense or
worried, or find your thoughts racing.

A Guided Visualization
of the Beach

You're walking down a long wooden stairway to a
beautiful, expansive beach. It looks almost
deserted and stretches off into the distance as
far as you can see. The sand is very fine and

light…almost white in appearance. You step onto the sand in your bare feet and rub it between your toes. It feels so good to walk slowly along this beautiful beach.

The roaring sound of the surf is so soothing that you can just let go of anything on your mind. You're watching the waves ebb and flow…they are slowly coming in…breaking over each other… and then slowly flowing back out again. The ocean itself is a very beautiful shade of blue…a shade of blue that is so relaxing just to look at.

You look out over the surface of the ocean all the way to the horizon, and then follow the horizon as far as you can see, noticing how it bends slightly downward as it follows the curvature of the earth. As you scan the ocean, you can see, many miles offshore, a tiny sailboat skimming along the surface of the water. All these sights help you just let go and relax even more.

As you continue walking down the beach, you become aware of the fresh, salty smell of the sea air. You take in a deep breath...breathe out...and feel very refreshed and even more relaxed. Overhead, you notice two seagulls flying out to sea...looking very graceful as they soar into the wind...and you imagine how you might feel yourself if you had the freedom to fly.

You find yourself settling into a deep state of relaxation as you continue walking down the beach. You feel the sea breeze blowing gently against your cheek and the warmth of the sun overhead penetrating your neck and shoulders. The warm, liquid sensation of the sun just relaxes you even more...and you begin to feel perfectly content on this beautiful beach. It's such a lovely day.

In a moment, up ahead, you see a comfortable-looking beach chair. Slowly, you begin to approach the beach chair...and when you finally reach it, you sit back and settle in.

Lying back in this comfortable beach chair, you let go and relax even more, drifting even deeper into relaxation.

In a little while, you might close your eyes and just listen to the sound of the surf, the unending cycle of waves ebbing and flowing. The rhythmic sound of the surf carries you even deeper...deeper still...into a wonderful state of quietness and peace.

Practice Meditation

Meditation is the one process that allows you to completely stop, let go of thoughts about the immediate past or future, and simply focus on being in the here and now.

Here are some basic guidelines for practicing meditation, followed by exercises for using a mantra, or meditative phrase, and for using the breath in meditation.

- Find a quiet environment. Do what you can to reduce external noise. If this is not possible, play soft instrumental sounds, or sounds from nature.

- Reduce muscle tension. If you're feeling tense, spend some time relaxing your muscles.

- Sit properly. Sit in either of the following two positions. Eastern style: Sit cross-legged on the floor with a cushion or pillow supporting your buttocks. Rest your hands on your thighs. Lean slightly forward so that some of your weight is supported by your thighs as well as your buttocks. Western style (preferred by most Americans): Sit in a comfortable, straight-backed chair, with your feet on the floor and legs uncrossed, hands on your thighs.

- In either position, keep your back and neck straight without straining to do so.

- Make it a regular practice to meditate every day. Even if you meditate for only five minutes, it's important to do it every day.

- Don't meditate on a full stomach or when you are tired. Select a focus for your attention. The most common devices are your own breathing cycle or a mantra (which we'll explain).

- Assume a nonjudgmental, passive attitude. Concentrate on whatever you've chosen as an object of meditation but don't

force or strain yourself to do so.
When distracting thoughts or
daydreams emerge, attempt
neither to hold on to them nor
to reject them too vigorously.
Just allow them to come and go.
Then bring your attention back
to your object of focus.

- Let go. Refrain from trying to
  do anything other than gently
  guiding your attention back to
  your object of focus. The more
  you let go, the deeper your
  meditation will be.

Meditate Using a Mantra

- Select a word to focus on. It can be an English word such as "calm," "peace," or "one," or a Sanskrit mantra such as "Om Shanti," "Sri Ram," or "Om Nameh Shivaya." "Now" is also a good choice because it tends to bring your focus into the present moment when said repeatedly.

- Repeat this word or phrase throughout your period of meditation, ideally on each exhalation.

- As any thoughts come to mind, just let them pass over and through you. Then gently bring your attention back to the repetitive word or phrase.

- Continue this process for a minimum of ten minutes.

Counting Down Breaths

- As you sit quietly, focus on the inflow and outflow of your breath. Each time you breathe out, count your breath. Begin with "twenty" and slowly count backward on each breath (20, 19, 18, etc.) down to zero, and then start over. Repeat the entire countdown process two or three times. Alternatively, you can simply repeat the word "one" on each exhalation for a period of ten minutes.

- Each time your focus wanders, bring it back to your breath and counting. If you get caught in an internal monologue or fantasy, don't worry about it or judge yourself. Just relax and return to the count again.

- If you lose track of the count, start over at "twenty" and begin counting down again.

- After practicing breath-counting meditation for a while, you may want to let go of the counting and just focus on the inflow and outflow of your breathing cycle. The purpose of the counting is only to aid your concentration.

- Continue this process for a minimum of ten minutes.

Most people find that it takes persistent and disciplined effort over a period of several months to become proficient at meditating. Even though meditation is the most demanding of relaxation techniques, it is, for many people, the most rewarding.

Listen to Calming Music

Music has often been called the language of the soul. It seems to touch something deep within us. It can move you into inner spaces beyond your anxiety and worries. Relaxing music can help you settle down into a place of serenity deep within that is impervious to the stresses and problems of daily life. It may also uplift you from a depressed mood. Whether you use music while driving, as a background while at work, or in the foreground when you want to take time out to relax, it is one of the most powerful and time-honored methods for letting go of anxiety or worry. If you use music to assuage anxiety, be sure to select pieces that are genuinely relaxing rather than stimulating or emotionally evocative.

3

THINK
REALISTICALLY

The truth is that it's what we say to our-selves in response to any particular situation that mainly determines our mood and feelings. Often, we say it so quickly and automatically that we don't even notice, and so we get the impression that the external situation "makes" us feel the way we do. But it's really our interpretations and thoughts about what is happening that form the basis of our feelings.

In short, you are largely responsible for how you feel (barring physiological determinants, such as illness). This is a profound and very important truth—one that sometimes takes a long time to fully grasp. It's often much easier to blame the way you feel on something or someone outside yourself than to take responsibility for your reactions.

Yet it is through your willingness to accept that responsibility that you begin to take charge and have mastery over your life.

The realization that you are mostly responsible for how you feel is empowering once you fully accept it. It's one of the most important keys to living a happier, more effective, and anxiety-free life.

Catastrophizing

Fearful thinking takes many forms, but anxiety sufferers are often intimately acquainted with *catastrophizing*. When you catastrophize, you imagine that some disaster is imminent. You predict dire consequences from unremarkable occurrences: a small leak in the sailboat means it will surely sink, feeling tired and fatigued often means that you have cancer, a slight downturn in the economy means you'll soon be jobless and out on the street.

Like all anxious thoughts, catastrophic thoughts usually start with the words "what if": "What if I break my leg skiing?" "What if my plane is hijacked?" "What if my son starts taking drugs?" "What if I'm in a car wreck?" "What if I flunk the exam and have to drop out of school?" "What if they see me panic and think I'm crazy?" There are no limits to a really fertile catastrophic imagination.

Catastrophizing relies on an *overestimation* of the odds of a bad outcome as well as an *underestimation* of your ability to cope with it should it befall you. What are the odds, really, that your fatigue is caused by cancer? What really is the likelihood that your son is taking drugs or that you'll break your leg skiing? Suppose the worst did happen. Would you really be unable to cope? People survive difficult, even dire, situations all the time. Many of us know someone who's overcome a bout with cancer or trouble with a child. Certainly, these experiences would be difficult, undesirable, and trying, but what are the odds really that you could not weather them?

The following four steps are essential for challenging catastrophizing and undermining its power over you:

- Notice the catastrophic thought pattern.

- Identify the distorted thoughts.

- Question their validity.

- Replace them with more realistic thoughts.

Here's an example of how you might challenge catastrophizing over a fear of serious illness. Other examples can be found at www.newharbinger.com/47612.

Notice the Catastrophic Pattern of Thought

"I have no energy and feel tired all the time. What if I have cancer and don't know it? If I were diagnosed with cancer, that would be the end. I couldn't take it. I'd be better off ending things quickly and killing myself."

Identify the Distorted Thoughts The distorted thoughts are "Because I have low energy and feel tired, I must have cancer" and "If I had cancer, I certainly couldn't cope." In identifying distorted thoughts, first list all of your what-ifs about the situation, then change them to affirmative statements. For example, "What if my low energy and fatigue are signs of cancer?" would get changed to "Because I have low energy and fatigue, I have cancer."

Question the Thoughts' Validity "What are the odds that low energy and fatigue mean that I have cancer? If the unlikely happened and I really was diagnosed with cancer, how terrible could that be? Would I actually go to pieces and not be able to continue living? Realistically, is it true that I would have no way of coping with the situation?" In challenging the validity of your catastrophic thoughts, it's helpful to use questions like these: "What are the odds?" "Realistically, how likely is that?" "How often has that happened in the past?" "If the worst did happen, is it really true that I'd not find any way to cope?"

Replace Distorted Thoughts with More Realistic Ones "Symptoms of fatigue and low energy can be indicative of all kinds of physical and psychological conditions. There are many possible explanations for my condition, and I don't have any specific symptoms that would indicate cancer. So the odds of my fatigue and low energy indicating cancer are very low. Moreover, as bad as a cancer diagnosis would be, it's unlikely that I would totally go to pieces. It would certainly be difficult, but I wouldn't be less equipped to handle it than anyone else."

Now it's your turn. Below are the guidelines for challenging fearful thoughts.

Following the guidelines, you will find a section of journaling prompts that will allow you to challenge fearful thoughts.

- Pick a time when you're relatively relaxed and calm, preferably not in the middle of an episode of intense anxiety or worry.

- After you get somewhat relaxed, ask yourself, "What was I telling myself that made me anxious?" Think of all the what-if thoughts you were telling yourself and write them under the first subhead on the worksheet: What I Was Telling Myself.

- To make your distorted thoughts clearer and easier to challenge, change them from what-if statements to regular, affirmative statements. It is easier to see the distortion when you change a what-if thought like "What if this plane crashes" to the definite statement "This plane is going to crash." Write your revised thoughts under the second subhead on the worksheet: My Distorted Patterns of Thought.

- Challenge your distorted thoughts by asking questions such as these: "What are the realistic odds of this happening?" "How often has this happened in the past?" "Am

I viewing this situation as completely unmanageable or unsurvivable?" Write these challenges under the subhead: Challenging My Distortions

- Use the questions to come up with more realistic thoughts about the situation or worry. Write these realistic thoughts under the subhead: More Realistic Thought Patterns.

- Finally, think about ways you could cope if your worst fear happened. Ask yourself, "If the worst happened, what could I do to cope?" In most cases, this will help you to see that you under-estimate your ability to cope. Write your ways of coping under the subhead: If the Worst Did

Happen, What I Could Do to Cope.

- Reread the realistic thoughts and ways you could cope with the worst-case scenario many times over a few weeks. This will reinforce them strongly in your mind. You might want to rewrite these statements on an index card that you keep with you and can pull out at a moment's notice.

- Repeat all of the steps of this exercise, using a separate copy of the worksheet, for each of your fears or worries.

Replacing Distorted Thoughts with Realistic Ones

In a separate journal or piece of paper, work through one of your distorted, fearful thoughts using the following prompts. (Or you can visit www.newharbinger.com/47612 and download the Realistic Thoughts Worksheet. Make copies: the exercise is most effective if you do it repeatedly as the fearful thoughts arise.)

What I Was Telling Myself

My Distorted Patterns of Thought

Challenging My Distortions

More Realistic Thought Patterns

If the Worst Did Happen, What I Could Do to Cope

Other Distorted Patterns of Thought

Catastrophizing is not the only pattern of distorted thinking that can trigger anxiety. Here are seven others. Which do you recognize?

Filtering You focus on the negative details while ignoring all the positive aspects of a situation.

Polarized Thinking Things are black or white, good or bad. You have to be perfect or you're a failure. There's no middle ground, no room for mistakes.

Overgeneralization You reach a general conclusion based on a single incident or piece of evidence. You exaggerate the frequency of problems and use negative global labels. This pattern can lead to an increasingly restricted life.

Mind Reading Without their saying so, you just "know" what people are feeling and why they act the way they do. In particular, you have certain knowledge of how people think and feel about you. You're afraid to actually check it out with them.

Magnifying You exaggerate the degree or intensity of a problem. You turn up the volume on anything bad, making it loud, large, and overwhelming. The flip side of magnifying is minimizing. When you view your assets, such as your ability to cope and find solutions, you look through the wrong end of the telescope so that everything positive is minimized. This pattern creates a tone of doom and hysterical pessimism, which easily gives way to anxiety.

Personalization You assume that everything people do or say is some kind of reaction to you. You also frequently compare yourself to others, trying to determine who is smarter, more competent, better looking, and so on.

Shoulds You have a list of ironclad rules about how you and other people should act. People who break the rules anger you, and you feel guilty when you violate the rules. "I should be the perfect friend, parent, teacher, student, or spouse," "I should know, understand, and foresee everything," "I should be nice and never display anger," and "I should never make mistakes" are examples of unrealistic "shoulds."

The following exercise is designed to help you notice and identify distorted thinking patterns. Read each statement carefully and refer back to the above summary to see how each statement or situation is based on one or more forms of distorted thinking.

Recognizing the Patterns

- The washing machine breaks down. A mother with twins in diapers says to herself, "This always happens. I can't stand it. The whole day's ruined."

- "He looked up from across the table and said, 'That's interesting.' I knew he was dying for breakfast to be over so he could get away from me."

- A man was trying to get his girlfriend to be warmer and more supportive. He got irritated every night when she didn't ask him how his day was or failed to give him the attention he expected.

- A driver feels nervous on long trips, afraid of having car trouble or getting sick and being stranded far from home. Faced with having to drive 500 miles to Chicago and back, he tells himself, "It's too far. My car has over 60,000 miles on it—it'll never make it."

- Getting ready for the prom, a high school student thinks, "I've got the worst hips in my homeroom, and the second-worst hair...If this French twist comes undone, I'll just die."

(Answers: 1. overgeneralization, filtering; 2. mindreading; 3. shoulds; 4. catastrophizing, magnifying; 5. personalization, polarized thinking, catastrophizing.)

Seven Solutions for Seven Distortions

Here are some useful methods for balancing the distorted patterns of thought that spark anxiety.

Filtering In order to conquer filtering, you will have to deliberately shift focus. You can shift focus in two ways. First, focus on the solution instead of the problem. Place your attention on coping strategies for dealing with the problem, rather than obsessing about the problem itself. Second, focus on the opposite of your primary mental theme, which, with anxiety, is danger or insecurity. Focus instead on things in your environment that represent comfort and safety. A classic question to ask with all forms of filtering is "Am I seeing the glass half empty or half full?"

Polarized Thinking The key to overcoming polarized thinking is to stop making black-or-white judgments. Think in terms of percentages: "About 30 percent of me is scared to death, and 70 percent is holding on and coping."

Overgeneralization Overgeneralization is exaggeration—the tendency to take a button and sew a vest on it. Fight it by quantifying instead of using words like *huge, awful, massive, minuscule*, and so on. For example, if you catch yourself thinking, "We're buried under massive debt," rephrase with a quantity: "We owe $27,000."

Mind Reading In the long run, you are probably better off making no inferences at all about people's internal thoughts. Either believe what they tell you or hold no belief at all until some conclusive evidence comes your way. Treat all of your notions about people as hypotheses to be tested and checked out by asking them.

Magnifying To combat magnifying, stop using words like *terrible, awful, disgusting,* or *horrendous.* In particular, banish phrases like "I can't stand it," "It's impossible," or "It's unbearable." You can stand it, because history shows that human beings can survive almost any psychological blow and endure incredible physical pain. Try saying to yourself phrases such as "I can cope" and "I can survive this."

Personalization When you catch yourself comparing yourself to others, remind yourself that everyone has strong and weak points. By matching your weak points to other people's corresponding strong points, you are just looking for ways to demoralize yourself. If you assume that the reactions of others are often about you, force yourself to check it out.

Shoulds Reexamine and question any personal rules or expectations that include the words should, ought, have to, or must. Flexible rules and expectations don't use these words because there are always exceptions and special circumstances. Think of at least three exceptions to your rule, and then imagine all the exceptions there must be that you can't think of.

4

FACE YOUR FEARS

The most effective way to overcome a phobia is simply to face it. To someone struggling with phobia-related anxiety, this can seem like a stark declaration. In fact, if you just thought, "No way!," we're not surprised. But exposure is a gradual, step-by-step process, not a sudden immersion. You'll face your fears in small, even minute, increments.

For many people, anxiety stems from phobias. A phobia is an exaggerated fear of a particular situation or experience that causes your anxiety to spike. Usually, you avoid the situation. In some cases, even the thought of the feared situation is enough to trigger your anxiety. If you have a phobia, your anxiety does not come out of the blue. It is caused by the thought or the real possibility of being in a feared situation.

Phobias are developed by sensitization. This is a process of becoming overly sensitive (sensitized) to a particular stimulus. In the case of phobias, it involves learning to associate anxiety with a particular situation.

Exposure Therapy

Exposure therapy allows you to unlearn the connection between a particular situation or object and a conditioned anxiety response that you've previously acquired, resulting in a phobia. With exposure, you confront a phobic situation by completing a series of activities, called a hierarchy, that brings you incrementally, but ultimately, into the situation you fear. Exposure therapy involves both of these elements:

- Unlearning the connection between a phobic situation and a fearful response.

- Reassociating feelings of calmness and confidence with that particular situation.

For all its effectiveness, exposure isn't a particularly easy or comfortable process to go through. Not everyone is willing to tolerate the unpleasantness of facing phobic situations or to persist with doing so on a regular basis. Exposure therapy demands a strong commitment on your part. If you're genuinely committed to your recovery, then you'll be willing to:

- take the risk to start facing situations you may have been avoiding for many years;

- tolerate the initial discomfort that entering phobic situations— even in small increments—often involves; and

- persist in practicing exposure on a consistent basis, despite possible setbacks, over a long enough period of time to allow your complete recovery (generally, this can take from weeks to up to a year or more).

If you're ready to make a consistent commitment to exposure for as long as it takes, you will recover from your phobias.

Coping Exposure Versus Full Exposure

The exposure process can generally be divided into two stages: coping exposure and full exposure. The *coping exposure* stage involves relying on various supports to help you get started with exposure and negotiate the early steps in the process. Such supports might include a person to accompany you (referred to as a "support person"), a low dose of a tranquilizer, practicing deep abdominal breathing, or rehearsing positive "coping statements." (See, for example, the list of coping statements in chapter 10.) As you progress beyond the early steps of your hierarchy (an incremental series of approaches to your phobic situation), you need to gradually wean yourself away from such coping strategies.

The second, full exposure, stage follows. *Full exposure* means you enter into your phobic situation without relying on supports or coping strategies. Full exposure is necessary because it teaches you that you can handle a situation you previously avoided under any circumstances. Instead of learning "I can only handle driving on freeways if I take medication," you learn that "I can handle driving on freeways regardless of my anxiety or anything I might use to mitigate it." Full exposure leads to complete mastery of a previously phobic situation.

Some people courageously undertake full exposure without any coping strategies because it is the fastest and most efficient way to overcome a phobia. Other people prefer the gentler approach of utilizing coping strategies to help them get started with exposure and negotiate its early stages. Gradually, as they proceed, they wean themselves away from these coping strategies in order to fully master the situation.

Coping Versus Mastery Exposure

The distinction just made between "coping exposure" and "full exposure" implies that there are really two approaches to dealing with phobias: simply coping versus full mastery. Complete mastery of a phobia—for example, flying, riding elevators, or driving freeways—is definitely desirable. In actual practice, however, some people opt for simply coping—being able to negotiate their phobic situation with the use of whatever aids they feel they need. Their aim is just to cope with the situation, not to fully master it.

Doing the exposure over and over every single day for weeks and months on end will make full mastery (without need of supportive coping strategies) more achievable. Phobic situations you encounter rarely are different. If flying or giving a presentation is a relatively rare event, then reliance on whatever resource is needed just to cope with the situation may be sufficient for you (while others still seek full mastery over longer periods of time).

Creating an Exposure Hierarchy

Exposure therapy works by creating a hierarchy. This is a series of steps that bring you incrementally closer to being in your feared situation.

Write out your hierarchy on a sheet of paper or in your journal. (You can find examples of hierarchies for overcoming phobias at www .newharbinger.com/47612.)

Be sure to start off with a simple, only mildly anxiety-arousing step and work up to a final step that you would be able to do if you were fully recovered from your phobia. Create a hierarchy for both the "coping exposure" and "full exposure" phases, with five to ten steps that involve progressively more challenging exposures. Start with a relatively easy or mild instance of facing your fearful situation.

Exposure therapy means carrying out each step of your coping and full exposure hierarchy in real life. Practice each step until you feel only mild to moderate anxiety at most, then proceed to the next step. Again, keep practicing it until your anxiety diminishes to a range where you feel you can easily manage it.

Occasionally, it may be difficult to negotiate a particular step. You may, for example, be able to handle step 9, but become very anxious when you face step 10. In this instance, you need to construct an intermediate step (9½) that can serve as a bridge between the two original steps.

Next to each step in the hierarchy, note the date you complete it. When you've completed both your coping and full exposure hierarchies for your first goal, write another two hierarchies for your next goal, and so on.

Basic Exposure Practice

These two steps detail how to proceed as you practice exposure:

- Enter and endure the situation. Proceed into your phobic situation, beginning with the first step of your hierarchy or with the one at which you last left off. Stay in the situation even if your anxiety begins to feel somewhat uncomfortable. If your anxiety feels manageable, great. Just stay in your fearful situation and endure your anxiety. Even if you are uncomfortable in the situation, stay with it as long as your anxiety level does not go to the point where it begins to feel unmanageable or out of control.

- Continue working up your hierarchy. Work through your hierarchy step by step. If you have to retreat from and then return to a step, that's fine; just continue to proceed up the steps of your hierarchy during your exposure session for the day. Accept anxiety symptoms if they come up, and do your best to endure them as they arise and pass. Do not chastise yourself if your performance turns out to be less spectacular than it was initially.

In general, longer exposure sessions achieve more rapid results than short sessions do, but go at your own pace. For most people, one practice session per day, three to five days per week, is enough.

What If You Start to Panic During Coping Exposure?

Some anxiety experts advocate continuing to expose yourself to a phobic situation no matter how high anxiety rises, even to the point of panic. The problem with this is that, if you actually progress to a full-blown panic attack during exposure, you could risk re-sensitizing yourself to the situation and rein-forcing your fear of the phobia.

This is particularly true during the early, coping phase of exposure. While it's always best to try to endure the discomfort you feel with exposure, it's also helpful to be able to have an "exit strategy" if a full-blown panic attack seems imminent. If you suddenly feel you're heading toward a full-blown panic attack, consider temporarily retreating from the situation and then returning to it as soon as possible after your anxiety settles down to manageable proportions.

During the full exposure stage, most often you are sufficiently accustomed to the situation that a full-blown panic attack is unlikely to occur. In the unlikely instance that you start to panic during full exposure, you can choose to stop the exposure temporarily. Give yourself a few minutes to recover, but don't go home. Once you are calmer, finish the exposure session. Also, it's optimal if you can repeat an exposure to the same situation within the next day or two.

For more tips on making the most of exposure, visit www.newharbinger.com/47612.

Maintaining the Right Attitude

Approaching fearful situations with the right attitude is as important as (if not more important than) learning specific strategies for exposure. The following attitudes are particularly important in increasing your ability to effectively face and overcome your fears.

- Accept bodily symptoms of anxiety. Refrain from fighting or running away from your anxiety during exposure.

- Stay grounded in the present moment. Anxiety begins as a physical reaction and is aggravated further by "what-if" or catastrophic thoughts. The more you can stay grounded in your body in the present moment, the less you'll be carried away by such thoughts. During the coping phase of exposure, abdominal breathing is an excellent way to stay grounded in your body.

- Know that fear always passes. No state of anxiety is permanent—it always passes. The body metabolizes excess adrenaline in five to ten minutes, so the worst degree of panic you might ever experience is not likely to last beyond this.

- If you're anxious in the situation, you're already beginning exposure. When you face something you fear, you almost inevitably experience some anxiety. Every time your anxiety recurs, you can confidently remind yourself you are a step closer to being done with it.

- Exposure always works—with practice. There is no fear that cannot be overcome by repeated exposure. Exposure always defeats fear, if you're willing to persevere with facing what you fear again and again.

Imagery Exposure

Certain types of phobias are difficult to face in real life because of infrequent opportunities for direct exposure, such as thunderstorms or transcontinental flights. In such cases, rather than using traditional imagery desensitization, video exposures (for example, watching videos of lightning and thunderstorms) or high-tech reenactments of the situation called "virtual exposure" (for an explanation, see chapter 1 of *The Anxiety & Phobia Workbook*, sixth edition) are used.

In some cases, you may find it useful to visualize entering your phobic situation in imagery before you face it in real-life exposure. This provides a gentler way to deal with the situation initially before you confront it directly.

For more detailed information on imagery exposure, see our website, Helpforanxiety.com.

5

GET REGULAR
EXERCISE

Regular, vigorous exercise is one of the most powerful and effective methods of reducing anxiety. When you experience anxiety, your body's natural fight-or-flight reaction—the sudden surge of adrenaline in response to a threat—becomes excessive. Exercise is a natural outlet for your body when it is in the fight-or-flight mode of arousal. Regular exercise also diminishes the tendency to experience anticipatory anxiety toward phobic situations, expediting recovery from all kinds of phobias.

Muscles aren't the only thing exercise strengthens. Regular exercise has a direct impact on several physiological factors that underlie anxiety. Here are some of these physiological benefits:

- reduced skeletal muscle tension, which is largely responsible for

your feelings of being tense or
"uptight"

- more rapid metabolism of excess
  adrenaline and thyroxin in the
  bloodstream, the presence of
  which tends to keep you in a
  state of arousal and vigilance

- discharge of pent-up frustration,
  which can aggravate phobic
  reactions

- enhanced oxygenation of the
  blood and brain, which increases
  alertness and concentration

- stimulation of the production of
  endorphins, natural substances
  that resemble morphine in both
  their chemical makeup and their
  effect on your sense of
  well-being

- increased brain levels of serotonin (an important neurotransmitter), helping to offset both depressed moods and anxiety

- lowered pH (increased acidity) of the blood, which increases your energy level

- improved circulation and digestion

- improved elimination (from skin, lungs, and bowels)

- decreased cholesterol levels and blood pressure

- weight loss as well as appetite suppression in many cases

- improved blood sugar regulation (in the case of hypoglycemia)

Several psychological benefits accompany these physical shifts. These include the following:

- increased subjective feelings of well-being and self-esteem

- reduced dependence on alcohol and drugs

- reduced insomnia and depression

- improved concentration and memory

- greater sense of control over anxiety

Getting Ready for an Exercise Program

Certain physical conditions limit the amount and intensity of exercise you should undertake. Ask yourself the questions below before launching a program of regular exercise.

- Has your physician ever said you have heart trouble?

- Do you frequently have pains in your heart or chest?

- Do you often feel faint or have spells of dizziness?

- Has your physician ever told you that you have a bone or joint problem (such as arthritis) that has been or might be aggravated by exercise?

- Has a physician ever said that your blood pressure was too high?

- Do you have diabetes?

- Are you over forty years old and unaccustomed to vigorous exercise?

- Is there a physical reason, not mentioned here, why you should not undertake an exercise program?

If you answered no to all of the above questions, you can be reasonably assured that you are ready to start an exercise program. Begin slowly and increase your activity gradually over a period of weeks. It might be helpful to have a support person exercise with you initially.

Exercise to Meet Your Needs

Exercise needs to be of sufficient regularity, intensity, and duration to have a significant impact on anxiety. Ideally, the exercise is aerobic and performed four or five times a week for twenty to thirty minutes or more per session. Avoid exercising only once per week. Engaging in infrequent spurts of exercise is stressful to your body and generally does more harm than good. (Walking is an exception.)

Which forms of exercise you select depends upon your objectives. For reducing anxiety, aerobic exercise is typically the most effective. Common aerobic exercises include running or jogging, freestyle swimming, aerobics classes, vigorous cycling, and brisk walking.

Beyond aerobic fitness, you may have other objectives in taking up exercise. If increased muscle strength is important, you may want to include weightlifting or isometric exercise in your program. (If you have a heart condition or angina, you should probably not engage in weightlifting or bodybuilding.) Exercise that involves stretching, such as dancing or yoga, is ideal for developing muscular flexibility and is a good complement to aerobic exercise. If you want to lose weight, jogging or cycling is probably most effective. If discharging aggression and frustration is important, you might try competitive sports. Finally, if you just want to get out into nature, then hiking or gardening would be appropriate. Rigorous hiking (as done by the Sierra Club, for example) can increase both strength and endurance.

Here are some of the more common types of aerobic exercise. Each type has its advantages and possible drawbacks.

Running Running is one of the best forms of exercise for losing weight, as it burns calories quickly. A three-mile jog (approximately thirty minutes) four or five times per week can go a long way toward diminishing your vulnerability to anxiety. Work up to a pace of one mile every twelve minutes. The downside to running is that, over a period of time, it can increase your risk of injury. You can minimize your risk of injury by getting proper shoes, running on soft surfaces, warming up before you begin, and alternating jogging with other forms of exercise.

Swimming Swimming is an especially good exercise because it uses so many different muscles throughout the body. Doctors usually recommend swimming to people with musculoskeletal problems, injuries, or arthritis, because it minimizes shock to the joints. It does not promote weight loss to the same degree as running, but it will help firm up your body.

Cycling Cycling has become a very popular form of aerobic exercise in recent years. While having many of the same benefits as jogging, it's less damaging to your joints. To achieve aerobic conditioning, cycling needs to be done vigorously—approximately fifteen miles per hour or more on a flat surface. When you undertake cycling, give yourself a few months to work up to a fifteen-miles-per-hour cruising speed, that is, a mile every four minutes.

Fitness Classes Most fitness classes consist of some mixture of stretching, aerobic training, and strength training exercises led by an instructor. The structured format of a fitness class may be an excellent way to motivate you to exercise. About forty-five minutes to an hour of exercise (including warm-up) three to five times per week is sufficient.

Walking Walking has advantages over all other forms of exercise. First, it does not require training—you already know how to do it. Second, it requires no equipment other than a pair of shoes and can be done virtually anywhere. The chances of injury are less than for any other type of exercise. Finally, it's the most natural form of activity. All of us are naturally inclined to walk. To make walking aerobic, aim for about one hour at a brisk enough pace to cover three miles. If you make walking your regular form of exercise, do it four or five times per week, preferably outdoors.

Let Go of Excuses

Do you notice a sudden boost in your creative powers when it comes to making excuses for not exercising? If so, you're not alone, but that doesn't mean you should succumb to these excuses and let them undermine your resolve. Below are some common excuses for avoiding exercise and ways to counter them.

"I don't have enough time." What you are really saying is that you're not willing to make time. The problem is not a matter of time but one of priorities.

"I feel too tired to exercise." What many nonexercisers fail to realize is that moderate exercise can actually overcome fatigue. Many people exercise in spite of feeling tired and find that they feel rejuvenated and reenergized afterward.

"Exercise is boring—it's no fun." Is it really true that all the activities listed earlier are boring to you? Have you tried out all of them? It may be that you need to find someone to exercise with in order to have more fun. Or perhaps you need to go back and forth between two different types of exercise to stimulate your interest.

"It's too inconvenient to go out somewhere to exercise." This is really no problem, as there are several ways to get vigorous exercise in the comfort of your home. Stationary bicycles and powered treadmills have become very popular. Fitness exercise at home is convenient and fun: there are many free or inexpensive programs online. Other indoor activities include jumping on a rebounder, calisthenics, using a rowing machine, or using a universal gym with adjustable weights. Or just put on some wild music and dance for twenty minutes.

"Exercise causes a buildup of lactic acid—doesn't that cause panic attacks?" It is true that exercise increases the production of lactic acid; however, regular exercise also increases oxygen turnover in your body. Oxygen turnover is the capacity of your body to oxidize substances it doesn't need, including lactic acid. Any increase in lactic acid produced by exercise will be offset by your body's increased capacity to remove it. The net effect of regular exercise is an overall reduction in your body's tendency to accumulate lactic acid.

"I'm over sixty—and that's too old to start exercising." Unless your doctor gives you a clear medical reason for not exercising, age is never a valid excuse.

"I'm too overweight and out of shape" or "I'm afraid I'll have a heart attack if I stress my body by exercising vigorously." If you have physical reasons to worry about stressing your heart, be sure to design your exercise program with the help of your physician.

Vigorous walking is a safe exercise for virtually everyone and is considered by some physicians to be the ideal exercise, as it rarely causes muscle or bone injuries. Swimming is also a safe bet if you're out of shape or overweight. The important thing is to be consistent and committed, whether your program involves walking for one hour every day or training for a marathon.

"I've tried exercise and it didn't work." The question to ask here is why it didn't work. Perhaps it is time for you to give yourself another chance to discover all the physical and psychological benefits of a regular exercise program.

Regular physical exercise is an essential component of the total program for overcoming anxiety, worry, and phobias presented in this book. If you combine regular, aerobic exercise with a program of regular, deep relaxation (see chapter 1), you are undoubtedly going to experience a substantial reduction in generalized anxiety. Exercise and deep relaxation are the two methods most effective for altering a hereditary bio-chemical predisposition to anxiety—the part of your anxiety that you came equipped with, rather than learned.

6

EAT RIGHT

Choices about what, when, how, and how much we eat and drink can have a tremendous impact on how well we cope with anxiety. In general, a balanced, moderate, regular diet of mostly whole foods is the best support for both mental and physical health. This chapter will touch on the ways caffeine, sugar, supplements, macronutrient balance, and blood sugar levels affect anxiety.

Caffeine Jitters

Caffeine consumption, particularly in the form of coffee drinking, is central to our culture and is even something of a rite of passage.

But while it is often viewed as a coping aid, caffeine in all its forms can spur physiological states that precipitate anxiety. Caffeine increases the level of the neurotransmitter norepinephrine in your brain, which leaves you alert and awake, and it heightens sympathetic nervous system activity and adrenaline output in the same way that stress does. Also, caffeine robs you of vitamin B_1 (thiamine), which is one of the so-called anti-stress vitamins. In short, too much caffeine can keep you in a chronically tense, aroused condition, leaving you more vulnerable to anxiety.

As a general rule, you should limit your total caffeine consumption to less than 100 milligrams per day to minimize its anxiety-stimulating effect. This translates into one cup of percolated coffee or one or two diet cola beverages, at most, per day.

Keep in mind, though, that there are tremendous individual differences in sensitivity to caffeine. As with any addictive drug, chronic caffeine consumption leads to increased tolerance and a potential for withdrawal symptoms. It's better to taper off gradually over a period of several months.

Hypoglycemia

The average American consumes 120 pounds of sugar a year. Because our bodies are not evolved or equipped to rapidly process large doses of sugar, a chronic imbalance in sugar metabolism often results. For some, this means high levels of blood sugar, or diabetes, the prevalence of which has skyrocketed in our time. For many more, though, the problem is the exact opposite: periodic dips in blood sugar that trigger a condition called *hypoglycemia*.

The symptoms of hypoglycemia tend to appear when your blood sugar drops below 50 to 60 milligrams per milliliter or when it drops suddenly from a higher to a lower level. Typically, this occurs about two to three hours after eating a meal. It can also occur simply in response to stress, since your body burns up sugar very rapidly under stress.

Some of the most common symptoms are of hypoglycemia are light-headedness, nervousness, trembling, unsteadiness or weakness, irritability, and palpitations.

Do these symptoms sound familiar? All of them are also anxiety symptoms! In fact, for some, anxiety reactions may actually be caused by hypoglycemia. Generally, the anxiety recedes after having something to eat, which causes blood sugar to rise. An informal, nonclinical way to diagnose hypoglycemia is to determine whether you have any of the above symptoms three or four hours after a meal, and whether they then go away as soon as you have something to eat.

If you suspect that you have hypoglycemia or have had it formally diagnosed, you may want to implement the dietary modifications outlined below. Doing so may result in less generalized anxiety and increased feelings of serenity. You may also notice that you are less prone to depression and mood swings.

- Eliminate, as much as possible, all types of simple sugar from your diet.

- Substitute fruits (other than dried fruits, which are too concentrated in sugar) for sweets. Avoid fruit juices or dilute them with an equal amount of water.

- Reduce or eliminate simple starches such as pasta, refined cereals, potato chips, white rice, and white bread. Substitute instead complex carbohydrates such as whole-grain breads and

cereals, vegetables, and brown
rice or other whole grains.

- Have a complex carbohydrate
  and protein snack halfway
  between meals to maintain a
  steadier blood sugar level. As an
  alternative to snacks between
  meals, you can try having four or
  five small meals per day that are
  no more than two to three hours
  apart.

Acid-Alkaline Balance

A dietary change toward vegetarianism can
promote a calmer, less anxiety-prone disposition. If you're used to eating meat, dairy,
cheese, and egg products, it is not necessary,
or even advisable, to give up all sources of
animal protein from your diet. Giving up red

meat alone, for example, or restricting your consumption of cow's milk (and using soy or rice milk instead) can have a noticeable and beneficial effect.

How can vegetarianism lead to a calmer disposition? Meat, poultry, dairy, cheese, and egg products, along with sugar and refined flour products, are all acid-forming foods. These foods are not necessarily acid in composition, but they leave an acid residue in the body after they are metabolized, making the body itself more acid. To maintain a proper acid-alkaline balance in the body, it helps to decrease consumption of acid-forming foods.

Prominent among alkaline foods are all vegetables; most fruits (except plums, raisins, and prunes); whole grains such as brown rice, millet, and buckwheat; and bean sprouts. Ideally, 50 to 60 percent of the calories you consume should come from these foods. Try including more of the alkaline foods in your diet and see if it makes a difference in the way you feel. Increasing the number of alkaline-forming foods in your diet should not lead you to reduce your protein intake.

More Protein, Fewer Carbs

Carbohydrates are used by the body to produce sugar or glucose, the form of sugar the body and brain use for fuel. In order to transport glucose to the cells, your pancreas secretes insulin. Eating high levels of carbohydrates means your body produces higher levels of insulin, and too much insulin has an adverse effect on some of the body's most basic hormonal and neuroendocrine systems, especially those that produce prostaglandins and serotonin.

In short, eating high amounts of sweets, cereals, breads, pastas, or even grains (such as rice) or starchy vegetables (such as carrots, corn, and potatoes) can raise your insulin levels to the point that other basic systems are thrown out of balance. The answer is not to eliminate complex carbohydrates but to reduce them proportionately to the amounts of protein and fat you consume, without increasing the total number of calories in your diet.

By doing this, you will not end up eating a diet that is too high in fat or protein. Instead, you will continue to eat fats and protein in moderation while decreasing the amount of carbohydrates you have in each meal relative to fat and protein. The optimal ratio may be 30 percent protein, 30 percent fat, and 40 percent carbohydrate, with vegetable sources of protein and fat preferable to animal sources.

Herbal and Vitamin Supplements

Herbs are plant-based medicines that have been an integral part of health care for thousands of years. In fact, about 25 percent of present-day prescription medications are still based on herbs.

Herbs tend to work more slowly and gently than prescription drugs. If you're used to the rapid and intense effects of a drug like Xanax, you need to be patient with the milder effect of a relaxing herb such as valerian. The principal advantage of herbs is that they work naturally, in harmony with your body, rather than imposing a specific biochemical change, as in the case of drugs.

Some herbs that have been found to be beneficial for relaxation and stress relief are kava, valerian, passionflower, and gotu kola.

While herbal treatments have advantages, it's important to remember that just because they are natural does not mean they're risk-free. Before trying any of the herbs mentioned above or any other herbal treatments, be sure to consult your physician.

Vitamin B-complex, vitamin C, and chelated chromium (such as chromium picolinate, often called glucose tolerance factor) can also help stabilize blood sugar. Vitamin B-complex and vitamin C are useful in increasing your resilience to stress.

7

NOURISH YOURSELF

Self-nourishment means maintaining a daily routine of sufficient sleep, recreation, and downtime. It also means pacing yourself through your day to allow time for such things. Taking time for self-nourishment provides you with the energy, presence of mind, and stamina that you need to pursue the activities and goals that make up your life. It also contributes to a calmer, more serene outlook, which is fundamental to reducing anxiety.

Some people see self-nourishment as a luxury that they can't readily afford. It is important to remember, though, that self-nourishment is not an optional adjunct to your daily schedule; it is essential to maintaining that schedule.

Take Downtime

Downtime is exactly what it sounds like—time out from work or other responsibilities to give yourself an opportunity to rest and replenish your energy. Without periods of downtime, any stress you experience while dealing with work or other responsibilities tends to become cumulative. It keeps building without any respite. Sleep at night doesn't count as downtime. If you go to bed feeling stressed, you may sleep for eight hours and still wake up feeling tense, tired, and stressed. The primary purpose of downtime is simply to allow a break in the stress cycle to prevent your stress from building. Optimally, you should have downtime at least one hour per day, one day per week, and one out of every twelve to sixteen weeks.

During periods of downtime, disengage from any task you consider work, put aside all responsibilities, and don't answer the phone unless you know it's someone you enjoy hearing from on the other end of the line.

There are three kinds of downtime: rest time, recreation time, and relationship time.

Rest time is time when you set aside all activities and just allow yourself to be. You stop action and let yourself fully rest. Rest time might involve lying on the couch and doing nothing, quietly meditating, sitting in your recliner and listening to peaceful music, or soaking in your bathtub. The key to rest time is that it is fundamentally passive; you allow yourself to stop doing and accomplishing and just be. Contemporary society encourages us to be productive and always accomplish more and more every moment of the waking day. Rest time is a needed counterweight.

Recreation time is time spent engaging in activities that help re-create you, that is, serve to replenish your energy. Recreation time brightens and uplifts your spirit. In essence, it is doing anything that you experience as fun or play.

Relationship time is time when you put aside your private goals and responsibilities in order to enjoy being with another person, or, in some cases, with several people. The focus of relationship time is to honor your relationship with your partner, children, extended family members, friends, or pets, and forget about your individual pursuits for a while.

Take some time to reflect on how you might allocate more time for each of the three types of downtime: rest time, recreation time, and relationship time. Write your answers in a journal or on a separate piece of paper.

Pace Yourself

Self-image and personal ideals frequently do not harmonize with the needs of the body. The degree of stress you experience today is a direct measure of how far you've gotten ahead of your body's needs in the past. Pacing yourself and giving yourself small breaks throughout the day are two ways to begin reversing unhealthy trends and living more in harmony with yourself.

Pacing means living your life at an optimal rate. Too much activity packed into each day, without breaks, leads to exhaustion, stress, anxiety, and perhaps even illness. Not enough activity leads to boredom and self-absorption. Many people with anxiety problems tend to pace themselves too fast, following the lead of a society that tells us to do more, achieve more, and excel no matter what the cost. Just as you wouldn't buy clothes to fit your neighbor, cousin, or spouse, you shouldn't design a schedule that might work for someone else, but not for you.

A higher level of relaxation and inner peace requires a schedule that allows for time between activities to rest, reflect, and simply be. If you tend to rush through the activities of your day, experiment with slowing down and giving yourself a five- to ten-minute minibreak every hour or at least every two hours. Minibreaks can be especially helpful at times when you transition from one activity to another.

Consider whether you might be a workaholic. *Workaholism* is an addictive disorder characterized by an unhealthy preoccupation with work. Those who suffer from it find that work is the only thing that gives them a sense of inner fulfillment and self-worth. You devote all your time and energy to work, neglecting both your physical and your emotional needs.

If you're a workaholic, or if you have workaholic tendencies, focus on learning to enjoy the nonwork aspects of your life and achieving a more balanced approach in general.

Sometimes you simply need to be willing to do less. That is, you are willing to literally reduce the number of tasks and responsibilities you handle in any given day. Consider how you can shift your values in the direction of placing more emphasis on the process of life (how you live) as opposed to accomplishments and productivity (what you actually do) within your current life situation. This is a good topic for exploring in a journal: take a break from reading and write about how you might be willing to do less.

Get a Good Night's Sleep

Healthy sleep patterns are a common casualty of the 24/7 pace of the modern world. To some, a good night's sleep is seen almost as a treat, but sufficient sleep is essential to your overall well-being. Lack of sleep can be both a cause and an effect of anxiety.

It's important to remember that sleep is as integral to physical and mental well-being as proper nutrition and regular exercise. Here are some guidelines to help you maintain a healthy sleep routine.

Do:

- Exercise during the day.

- Go to bed and get up at regular times.

- Develop a sleep ritual before bedtime. This is some activity you do nightly before turning in.

- Reduce noise. Use earplugs or a noise-masking machine, like a fan, if necessary.

- Block out excess light.

- Keep your room temperature between sixty-five and seventy degrees.

- Purchase a quality mattress.

- Have separate beds if your partner snores, kicks, or tosses and turns.

- Enjoy physically and emotionally satisfying sex.

- See a psychotherapist if necessary.

- Turn yourself down during the last hour or two of the day.

:   Avoid vigorous physical or
    mental activity, emotional
    upsets, and so on.

- Try a hot shower or bath before
  bedtime.

Don't:

- Try to force yourself to sleep. If
  you're unable to fall asleep after
  twenty to thirty minutes in bed,
  leave your bed, engage in some
  relaxing activity, and return to
  bed only when you're sleepy.

- Have a heavy meal before
  bedtime or go to bed hungry.

- Indulge in heavy alcohol
  consumption before bedtime.

- Have too much caffeine.

- Smoke cigarettes.

- Engage in nonsleep activities (except sex) in bed.

- Nap during the day.

- Let yourself be afraid of insomnia. Work on accepting those nights when you don't sleep so well.

Here are a few more tips for working on the quality of your sleep.

- With your doctor's or health practitioner's approval, try natural supplements that foster sleep. Do not exceed recommended doses and be sure to discuss all herbs with your doctor before taking them.

- For relaxing tense muscles or a racing mind, use deep relaxation techniques. Specifically, progressive muscle relaxation or taped guided visualization exercises can be helpful (see chapters 1 and 2).

- Try varying the firmness of your mattress.

- If pain is causing sleeplessness, try an analgesic. In the case of pain, this is more appropriate than a sleeping pill.

* * *

Although life brings ups and downs—even sudden, unexpected challenges—you can find reprieve from worry and build a sense of inner security through small acts of kindness toward yourself on a daily basis. Doing so requires first that you make time to nurture yourself apart from the responsibilities of work and household. Building a loving relationship with yourself is really not much different from developing a close relationship with someone else: both require some time, energy, and commitment. Giving yourself regular downtime is one way to do this.

8

SIMPLIFY YOUR LIFE

Having a life that is freighted with financial and time commitments, as well as excessive material items, is a modern source of anxiety. Although this kind of excess is characteristic of our time, it remains true that the simpler our lives, the richer our experience and the deeper our sense of well-being.

The simple life is free of those demands on your time and finances that deplete your resources without enriching your life in some way. It can be thought of as a lifestyle that yields a better return on your investment of time and money.

Elements of the Simple Life

There is no precise formula defining what constitutes living simply. Each individual is likely to discover his or her own ways to reduce complexity and unnecessary encumbrances.

There have been indications in recent years that an increasing number of people have favored simplifying their lives. After the economic recession that began in 2008, many people found it necessary to downsize and simplify their lives. However, the trend toward a more simplified lifestyle has been popular for more than twenty-five years.

Below are a few suggestions for simplifying your life. Some are changes you can make immediately, while others require more time and effort on your part. Remember that the goal of the simple life is to free yourself from commitments that deplete your time, energy, and money without meeting your essential needs or sustaining your spirit.

Downsize Your Living Situation There are several benefits of smaller living quarters. First, it is just not possible to accumulate a large number of possessions without sufficient room for them. Also, a smaller space takes less time to clean and maintain and is typically less expensive.

Let Go of Things You Don't Need It's easy to accumulate stuff that has no real value or use to us and only creates clutter. Take a look at your stuff and decide what is useful and worth keeping and what is simply taking up space. As a general rule, to reduce clutter, get rid of everything you haven't used in more than a year, except, of course, items that have sentimental value.

Do What You Want for a Living Doing what you truly want may require time, risk, and effort. It may take one to two years to gain the retraining or retooling you need to begin a new career. In our estimation—and that of others who have done it—the time, effort, and disruption are well worth it.

Reduce Your Commute Reducing or eliminating your commute is one of the most significant changes you can make in simplifying your life. It doesn't take much reflection to see the extent to which negotiating rush hour traffic on a daily basis can add to stress. Moving closer to where you work or choosing to live in a smaller town can help reduce your commute.

Reduce Exposure to the Screen Granted, there are many good programs on TV, and the internet is a wonderful tool for communicating information. While life in front of the screen can be a distraction from anxiety, it can also be a hindrance to rebuilding a deeper connection with nature, others, or yourself. If anxiety is aggravated by too much stimulation and an experience of disconnection on multiple levels, then it seems that spending time in front of the screen might be done in moderation.

Live Close to Nature Being in close proximity to the earth—its sights, sounds, smells, and energies—can help you remain more easily connected with yourself. Choosing to live in such a setting, if possible, allows you to reestablish an ongoing connection with the earth that much of modern civilization seems to have lost.

Tame the Telephone Many people feel they should answer the phone—landline or cell— virtually every time it rings, regardless of the time of day or the mood they're in at the time. Remember that answering the telephone is optional. You can let your voice mail pick up and return the call when you are ready to give the caller your full attention.

Delegate Menial Chores Even delegating one activity you don't like to do, such as house-cleaning or yard work, can make a difference in the sense of ease you bring to your day-to-day life. If money is an issue, is there something your children could learn to do just about as well as you? Perhaps you can allow other family members to help with the cooking, yard upkeep, or housecleaning.

Learn to Say No "No" is not a dirty word. Many people pride themselves on always being able to accommodate the needs and wants of their friends, family, and coworkers. The problem is that the end result of this consistent "helpfulness" is exhaustion. When someone asks you for your time, effort, or anything else, think about whether it serves both your highest interest and the other person's highest interest to respond with a "yes."

Simplify-Your-Life Questionnaire

Now it's your turn. Take some time to think about ways in which you might simplify your life. To help you do this, ask yourself the following questions.

- On a 1-to-10 scale, with 1 representing a high degree of simplicity and 10 representing a high degree of complexity, where would you rate your own lifestyle at present?

- Have you made any changes in your living arrangements in the past year toward simplicity? If so, what changes?

- What changes toward simplifying your life would you like to make in general?

- What changes toward simplifying your life are you willing to make in the next year?

9

GET OFF THE
WORRY SPIRAL

Obsessive worry often becomes a negative spiral that can easily end in anxiety. When you're locked in a spiral of obsessive worry, you tend to ruminate on every facet of a perceived danger until it eclipses all other thoughts and you feel trapped. Because obsessive worry can be very compelling, it takes a deliberate act of will to break out of it. You need to make a concerted effort to move away from the mental vortex of worry and shift to another mode of thought. Getting "out of your head" by doing or focusing on something outside yourself is an excellent way to halt the worry spiral. Although deliberately choosing to break out of obsessive worry may be difficult at first, with practice it gets easier.

Distract Yourself from Worry

Pulling yourself out of the worry spiral requires a change of focus from the cerebral to the practical. You need to become engaged in a project or an activity so that your concentration shifts from your fears of a possible, future danger to your strategies for completing the task at hand. Below is a list of ways to do this.

- Do physical exercise

- Talk to someone

- Do twenty minutes of deep relaxation

- Listen to emotionally meaningful music

- Experience something immediately pleasurable (such as a warm bath, funny movie, or back rub)

- Use visual distractions (such as TV or a movie)

- Express your creativity

- Find an alternative positive obsession that takes your focus (such as a puzzle or game)

- Repeat a positive affirmation

Defuse from Worry

Defusion describes a series of techniques derived from a form of therapy called acceptance and commitment therapy, or ACT for short. When you are "fused" with your thoughts, you tend to believe them as if they were absolute truth, even if they refer to some future danger that hasn't even happened (and isn't likely to).

The problem with fusion is that what you take to be absolutely true and real are simply strings of words and images in your head.

The way out is to stop believing everything you think.

Defusion is a process of disentangling from (ceasing to "fuse" with) unhelpful thoughts. When you defuse from thoughts, you recognize them for what they are—nothing more than a bunch of words and pictures "inside your head."

Defusion begins by simply asking yourself to notice what you're thinking. You might say to yourself:

- "Okay, so what is my mind telling me right now?"

- "What thoughts are going through my mind right now?"

- "Can I just notice what my mind is saying?"

- "What judgments am I making right now?"

Once you've identified your thoughts—perhaps even written them down—the next important question to ask is whether they are helpful or not—whether they work for you or not. In contrast with cognitive behavioral therapy, defusion is less concerned with the truth or falsity of a given thought than whether it's workable—whether it's helpful and leads to a richer, fuller, or more meaningful life (as opposed to leading to more stress and suffering).

Here are some common defusion techniques.

- Notice what your mind is telling you right now. Recall this question: "Okay, what is my mind telling me right now?"

- When you feel upset, notice your thoughts and write them down on an index card or piece of paper.

- Bracket a thought. Take a thought that you notice and preface it with the phrase "I'm having the thought that…"

- Imagine leaves on a stream. Imagine that you're sitting on the bank of gentle stream. Leaves have dropped into the stream and are floating by you. Now, for the next few minutes, take every thought that pops into your head, whether you like it or not, place it on a leaf, and let it flow by.

- Watch your thinking. Relax, center yourself in your body, and engage in abdominal breathing for one minute. Now shift your attention to your thoughts. Where are they? Where do they seem located in space? Are they inside your head? Are they floating around in "mental space" in your mind? Are they someplace else?

- Imagine a computer screen. Imagine your thoughts on a computer screen. Change the font, color, and format of them. Animate the words and images.

- Sing the thought. For example, take the thought "I'm a loser" and sing it to the tune of "Happy Birthday." (This is one of the more zany defusion techniques, which may or may not appeal to you, but it works for many people.)

- Consider the thought's workability. Ask yourself these questions: "If I go along with a particular thought, buy into it, and let it control me, where does that leave me?" "What do I get for buying into it?" "Does buying into that thought lead me to a better and more meaningful life?"

Worry Exposure

Worry exposure is a form of imagery exposure (see chapter 4) where you imagine in detail a worst-case scenario regarding a particular worry, say, for example, failing an exam or flubbing up a job interview or presentation.

The purpose is to repeatedly imagine the worrisome situation until you get bored or grow tired of it.

In order to do worry exposure, begin by imagining a worst-case scenario involving your particular worry. Write it up in detail. List all the aspects of the situation from start to finish. Be creative in writing a worst-case scenario and engage all of your senses, including sight, sound, touch, and even smell.

Note: If your initial worst-case scenario evokes excessive anxiety, then start with a milder worry and an easier scenario before proceeding to the most difficult one. However, for purposes of worry exposure, it's important that you feel some anxiety in response to imagining your scenario.

Use these steps when you practice worry exposure.

1. Relax and get comfortable.

2. Read the script of your worry scene slowly.

3. Close your eyes and visualize the scene for about ten to fifteen minutes. Go through it step by step, not as an outsider but as an active participant.

4. Practice step 3 several times over the course of a week for a set period of time from ten to twenty minutes.

5. After the timer goes off and you've completed a worry exposure session, spend a few minutes imaging an alternative scenario where the situation works out better. Be sure to wait until the exposure part is done before you imagine the alternative scenario.

Postpone Your Worry

Rather than trying to stop worry or obsessive thoughts altogether, you may opt to try postponing them for a bit. In a sense, you pay some credence to your worries or obsessive thoughts by telling them that you will only ignore them for a few minutes, but then you will attend to them later.

When you first try this technique, try postponing worry only for a short time, perhaps two or three minutes. Then, at the end of the allotted time, try postponing the worry again for a short time. When that period of time is up, set another specified time to postpone your worry. The trick is to keep postponing worry for as long as you can. Often you will be able to postpone a particular worry long enough that your mind moves on to something else.

Postponing worry is a skill that you can improve with practice. As with the other worry-disruption techniques, gaining skill with worry postponement will increase your confidence in your ability to handle all kinds of worries and obsessive thoughts.

Use Effective Action

Worrying about getting through a job interview, making a speech, or taking a long flight can be more stressful than the actual experience. That's because your body's fight-or-flight system makes no distinction between your fantasies about the situation and the situation itself. The simple process of developing such a plan will divert your mind away from the worry.

Make a Plan to Deal with Worry

Think about what worries you the most. Among your worries, which one has highest priority for you to take action on right now? If you are ready and willing to take action, follow this sequence of steps.

1. Write down the particular situation that is worrying you.

2. Make a list of possible things you can do to deal with and improve the situation. Write them down, even if they seem overwhelming or impossible to you right now. Ask family and friends for ideas as well.

3. Consider each idea. Which ones are not possible? Which ones are doable but difficult to implement?

Put a question mark after these. Which ones could you do in the next week to month? Put a check after these.

4. Make a contract with yourself to do all the things you checked off. Set specific dates for having them completed. When you have completed the checked items, go on to the more difficult things. Make a similar contract with yourself to do them and complete them by specific dates.

5. Are there any other items that originally looked impossible that you might be able to do now? If so, make a contract with yourself to do these, too—again completing them by specific dates.

6. Once you've fulfilled all of your contracts, ask yourself how the situation has changed. Has your worry been satisfactorily resolved? If the situation has not been resolved, go through this process again.

10

COPE ON THE SPOT

Resisting or fighting anxiety is likely to make it worse. It's important to avoid tensing up in reaction to anxiety or trying to make it go away. Acceptance of anxiety symptoms is the key. By cultivating an attitude of acceptance in the face of anxiety, you allow it to move through and pass. Anxiety is caused by a sudden surge of adrenaline. If you can let go and allow your body to have its reactions (such as heart palpitations, chest constriction, sweaty palms, and dizziness) caused by this surge, it will pass soon.

Acceptance of the initial symptoms of anxiety is very important, but then it's time to do something. When anxiety comes on, always accept it first, then realize that there are many things you can actively do to redirect the energy spent on the anxiety into something constructive. In short, don't try to fight with anxiety, but don't do nothing either.

To cope with anxiety in the moment, there are three types of recommended activities: (1) coping strategies, which are active techniques to offset anxiety or distract yourself from it; (2) coping statements, which are mental techniques designed to redirect your mind away from and replace fearful self-talk; and (3) affirmations, which can be used much like coping statements but are intended to work over a longer time period.

Use Coping Strategies

Coping strategies are quite useful for disrupting a panic attack at an early stage (that is, before it gains a lot of momentum), generalized anxiety (excessive worrying), or repetitive obsessive thoughts due to obsessive-compulsive disorder. The one situation where coping strategies are not recommended is when you are doing full exposure to a phobia in order to overcome it.

A number of coping strategies have already been covered in previous chapters. Beyond these, there are other active coping strategies that you might find helpful in dealing with all levels of anxiety, from worry and mild apprehension to panic. Some of the most popular strategies are described here.

Talk to a Supportive Person Nearby or on the Phone Talking to someone either in person or over your cell phone will help you get your mind off your anxious body symptoms and thoughts.

Move Around or Engage in Some Routine Activity Instead of resisting the normal physiological arousal that accompanies anxiety, you move with it. Taking a walk, doing household chores, or gardening are excellent ways to channel the physical energy of an anxiety reaction.

Stay in the Present Staying in the present and focusing on external objects will help minimize the attention you give to troublesome physical symptoms or catastrophic "what-if" thoughts. If possible, you might try actually touching objects nearby to reinforce staying in the immediate present.

Use Simple Distraction Techniques There are many simple, repetitive acts that can help distract your attention away from your anxiety. Here are some you can try:

- Unwrap and chew a piece of gum.

- Count backward from 100 in threes: 100, 97, 94, and so on.

- Count the number of people in line (or all of the lines) at the grocery store.

- Count the money in your wallet.

- While driving, count the bumps on the steering wheel.

- Snap a rubber band on your wrist. This may jar your mind out of anxious thoughts.

- Take a cold shower.

- Sing.

It bears repeating that distraction techniques are fine for helping you cope with the sudden onset of anxiety or worry. However, don't let distraction become a way of avoiding or running away from your anxiety.

Get Angry with Anxiety Getting angry and being anxious are incompatible responses. It's impossible to experience both at the same time. In some cases, it turns out that symptoms of anxiety are a stand-in for deeper feelings of anger or frustration. If you can get angry at your anxiety the moment it arises, you may stop it from building any further.

Time-honored techniques for physically expressing anger include

- pounding on a pillow on your bed with both fists

- screaming into a pillow—or in your car alone with the windows rolled up

- hitting a bed or a couch with a plastic baseball bat

- throwing eggs into the bathtub
  (the remains wash away)

- chopping wood

Please keep in mind that it's very important in expressing anger to direct it either into empty space or toward an object, not at another person. Rise above physical and verbal expressions of anger toward other human beings, especially those you love and care about.

Experience Something Pleasurable Just as anger and anxiety are incompatible responses, so the feeling of pleasure is incompatible with an anxiety state. Any of the following may help offset anxiety, worry, or even panic:

- Have your significant other or spouse hold you (or give you a back rub).

- Take a hot shower or relax in a hot bath.

- Have a pleasurable snack or meal.

- Engage in sexual activity.

- Read humorous books or watch a comical video.

Try a Cognitive Shift Thinking about any of the following ideas may help shift your point of view so that you can let go of worry or anxious thoughts:

- Acknowledge that it would be okay to lighten up about this.

- Turn the problem over to your Higher Power.

- Trust in the inevitability of it passing. Affirm "this too will pass."

- Realize that it's not likely to be as bad as your worst thoughts about it.

- Realize that working with the problem is part of your path to healing and recovery.

- Remember not to blame yourself. You're doing your best, and that's the best anyone can do.

- Expand your compassion for all people who experience similar anxiety. Remember you're not alone.

Use Coping Statements

Coping statements are designed to redirect—and retrain—your mind away from fearful, "what-if" self-talk toward a more confident and comfortable stance in response to anxiety. With repeated practice over time, you'll eventually internalize your coping statements to the point that they automatically come to mind when you find yourself confronted with anxiety or worry.

Here are some coping statements for preparing to face a fearful situation:

- Today I'm willing to go just a little outside my comfort zone.

- This is an opportunity for me to learn to become comfortable with this situation.

- Facing my fear of _____ is the best way to overcome my anxiety about it.

- Each time I choose to face _____, I take another step toward becoming free of fear.

- By taking this step now, I'll eventually be able to do what I want.

- There's no right way to do this. Whatever happens is fine.

Here are some coping statements for entering a fearful situation:

- I've handled this before and I can handle it now.

- Relax and go slowly. There's no need to push right now.

- Nothing serious is going to happen to me.

- It's okay to take my time with this. I'll do only as much as I'm ready to do today.

- I'm going to be all right. I've succeeded with this before.

Here are some coping statements for feelings of being trapped:

- Just because I can't leave right now doesn't mean I'm trapped. I'll relax for now, then leave in a while.

- The idea of being trapped is just a thought. I can relax and let go of that thought.

Here are some general coping statements for anxiety or panic:

- I can handle these symptoms or sensations.

- These sensations (feelings) are just a reminder to use my coping skills.

- I can take my time and allow these feelings to pass. I deserve to feel okay right now.

- This is just adrenaline—it will pass in a few minutes.

- This will pass soon.

- I can ride this through.

- These are just thoughts—not reality.

Put Your Coping Statements on Cards So that your coping statements are readily available, it's a good idea to put your favorite ones on an index card (or several cards, if you prefer), which you can keep in your purse or wallet, or tape to the dashboard of your car. Whenever you feel symptoms of anxiety coming on, bring out the card and read it. Remember, you need to practice your coping statements many times before you'll fully internalize them.

Use Affirmations

Coping statements, along with the coping strategies discussed earlier, can help diminish anxiety in the moment. Affirmations can be in the moment but are also useful long term. They can help you change long-standing beliefs that tend to perpetuate anxiety. Their purpose is to help you cultivate a more constructive and self-empowering attitude toward your own experience of anxiety.

Affirmations are intended to help you change the core attitudes and beliefs that contribute to your anxiety. Rehearsing them daily for a few weeks or months will begin to help you change your basic outlook about fear in a constructive direction.

Here are some example affirmations to try:

- Let it go.

- These are just thoughts—they're fading away.

- I am learning not to feed my worries—to choose peace over fear.

- When I see most situations as they truly are, there is nothing to be afraid of.

- I'm whole, relaxed, and free of worry.

YOUR ANXIETY TOOL KIT

When anxiety is overwhelming you, see chapter 10 for quick coping strategies. Use this space to list your most effective new skills and practices (including their page numbers in this book), so you can find and use them quickly and easily.

_____

_____

_____

_____

_____

_____

_____

_____

_____

_____

_____

_____

_____

_____

_____

_____

Edmund J. Bourne, PhD, has specialized in the treatment of anxiety, phobias, and other stress-related disorders for over two decades. His self-help books have helped over a million people, and have been translated into numerous languages. He currently resides in Florida and California.

Phone counseling for problems with panic attacks, phobias, and other anxiety difficulties is available with Edmund Bourne. For information, please call 1-415-686-7516. Further information about Bourne's work in the anxiety disorders field may be found at helpforanxiety.com.

For Edmund Bourne's work outside the field of anxiety disorders, please see his website, journeysofthemind .net.

Lorna Garano is a freelance writer and publicist.

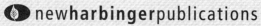

Real change *is* possible

For more than forty-five years, New Harbinger has published proven-effective self-help books and pioneering workbooks to help readers of all ages and backgrounds improve mental health and well-being, and achieve lasting personal growth. In addition, our spirituality books offer profound guidance for deepening awareness and cultivating healing, self-discovery, and fulfillment.

Founded by psychologist Matthew McKay and Patrick Fanning, New Harbinger is proud to be an independent, employee-owned company. Our books reflect our core values of integrity, innovation, commitment, sustainability, compassion, and trust. Written by leaders in the field and recommended by therapists worldwide, New Harbinger books are practical, accessible, and provide real tools for real change.

 **newharbinger**publications